My Love for Jesus and the American Spirit

Song Potpourri, Song Lyrics, and Poetry

Frank Easterling

ISBN 979-8-89243-428-7 (paperback)
ISBN 979-8-89243-429-4 (digital)

Christian Faith Publishing
832 Park Avenue
Meadville, PA 16335
www.christianfaithpublishing.com

Printed in the United States of America

To my Lord and Savior Jesus, my king Yahweh Shepherd.

To my family—my wife, Beverly, and children, Jason and Christina

My son Thomas Easterling, ten years old, and my dad Thomas B. Easterling III were lost in a house of fire in 1989.

My dad was a soldier. Barbara Easterling is my mother, whose maiden name is Jordan.

Thomas B. Easterling III

He receive the following awards:

South Vietnam Award
Purple Heart
Jungle Expert
Bronze Star with valor
Cross of Gallantry
Master Jumper (over three hundred jumps)
Retired E-8 for over twenty-seven years plus the reserve service

Contents

Introduction..vii

Chapter 1: King of Six Strings..1

Chapter 2: The Calling of a Soldier 2

Chapter 3: No Joke for Anyone 3

Chapter 4: God and Country...4

Chapter 5: Junk Food Junkie..5

Chapter 6: Step Up...6

Chapter 7: Flags of Our Fathers 7

Chapter 8: Give Love...8

Chapter 9: Get Back Up 9

Chapter 10: I'm a Bowl of Tenderness.......................................10

Chapter 11: The Legend of a Cowboy 11

Chapter 12: "Stupid Today, Stupid Ever in Love".....................12

Chapter 13: USA Built by God..13

Chapter 14: Madness Energy, Oh, Dear....................................14

Chapter 15: Forgiveness on a Wing and a Prayer.....................15

Chapter 16: Meet Somewhere in the Middle.............................16

Chapter 17: Amazing Glory..17

Chapter 18: Engage in the American Spirit...............................18

Chapter 19: God's Sweet Word...19

Chapter 20: Tip-Tap, Tip-Tap 20

Chapter 21: A Swing, Miss, No Kiss 21

Chapter 22: Words of Wisdom 22

Chapter 23: Hearts Eclipse 23

Chapter 24: Momma's Prayers..24

Chapter 25: Four Winds of Tide Blow In...................................25

Chapter 26: Notebook Diaries...26

Chapter 27: Talent for Two 27

Chapter 28: He's Always There 28

Chapter 29: Two Lifestyles...29

Chapter 30: Paper Bill of Rights 30

Introduction

This book is a testament to expressing my God-given talent for God's glory, reaching out to the troubled world, expressing my love for Jesus and the American Spirit, and connecting with my fans and friends.
Best wishes. Thanks.

Chapter 1

King of Six Strings

Pulling the strings to sing, guitar-picking man. You got an ear, like a suction cup. Nothing gets by you.

You can peel a note.

Feel a note in the air. You pick; you are Dick. The Guitar Man, you jam like Spam.

Fast Finger's, you're slick. You like the notes and split them. My, my, my, you got it going on and on.

You are the King of Six Strings. Shine on, shine on. Get down, slow and low. Low to high, you walk.

The strings to sing. Get Rhythm, get rhythm. Walk the scale to 4/4 beat and between 3/4 time.

You make it look natural, natural, guitar-picking man. (Dick jamming with Jim)

(Mike and whole bunch more cowboys and cowgirls.) King of Six Strings. Looking for a Queen of Six Strings, pulling the strings to sing.

Chapter 2

The Calling of a Soldier

A soldier, a trooper, airborne breed.

Seasoned for the mission as his commissioned officer gives the command, "Jump."

As he gives the signal of "thumbs up" high in the sky. Get ready, be ready, stay ready. The soldier replies, "Ready, sir." That's the motto a soldier lives by. "Lean and mean, ready for anything." Airborne specialists breed for the unknown to bring fear to the enemy. Surprise tactics encompass the enemy on the battlefield.

A soldier on a mission. The colors of the American flag fly in his heart.

To defend and serve. Touching many back home, a soldier, a trooper, airborne breed gets the job done—a hero. The calling of a soldier's sacrifice to serve, facing the unknown, ready for anything. Calling all soldiers, courage flows in their blood.

Thank God for soldiers one and all.

Chapter 3

No Joke for Anyone

Woke up dead, eyes closed for rest, facing fate, crossing over from receptive live sleep.

To waking up dead—woke up—living in HELL. Going from the thinkable to the unthinkable, facing the unimaginable.

God's warning about hellfire and brimstone. No dream from the price of sin.

Measures not taken in life to escape God's wrath for the wicked. Woke up dead, dreaded ransom for a lost soul.

Woke up dead, ready or not, roses of death. Your past choices have voices with consequential recourses. With no U-turns. Woke up dead, choking on smoke and fire. In the devil's den—lake of fire. Woke up dead, asking yourself how this could be.

I'm not dreaming,
I'm dancing with the dead,
In the devil's den.

Chapter 4

God and Country

Loving God and People. People loving God and Country. Opening Heaven's door of Grace.

Mercy with Hope for today and tomorrow,

Tomorrow thru Eternity. God's Love so amazing, undeniably touching the eclipse of God's blessings of our country. People, in return, reach out to God and their Country. Loving God and People

So right…oh-so-right.

People loving God and Country

(Can I get an AMEN!)

Chapter 5

Junk Food Junkie

I'M AS HIP AS I AM. I JAM LIKE Spam, LIKE PEANUT AND JELLY ON A SANDWICH.

I'M AS HIP as I am, with popcorn and Coke, Cake, and Ice Cream celebration.

Mmm, good! Can't get enough of pure junk food, taste buds of satisfaction.

Oh, yea! Yea, man! Oh, yea!

I'm classified as a junk food junkie. X2—that's my life, JUNK FOOD JUNKIE!

I'm as Hip as I am. I got to have it all—chips and salsa.

I like mine hot as it comes.

Chapter 6

Step Up

Someone, step up if you please. Somebody got to be rocking your boat.

The Thorn between two roses, two birds a sing a song with wings in the balance

Choices with voices, Echoes of Love, E-mails by the dozen secret admirers

Winds of emotion storm over me. Who could this be?

Hiding behind a curtain of betrayal, not willing to compromise.

But echoes of love are so strong, so inviting. It's hard to resist the temptations of a secret

Admirer going on and on again against my true first love. The thorn between two roses, something got to give.

Something has got to give. I've got to live out my passion; promises are in conflict. Reflection of my heart is torn

To the core of my heart.

Chapter 7

Flags of Our Fathers

True Soldiers of Armed Forces past and present (x2). Flags of our Fathers stand out in memory

Bleed out to lead, defend, feed our freedom of liberty. Ring the bell of honor. Ring the bell of honor

Liberty Bell rings loud and proud, declaring democracy with flags of our father's Red, White, and Blue; she may be old, but she's bold, so bold

Can't break her will to defend and fight with all her might; like the wings of an eagle, she soars. Flags of the fathers testify, stand out loud and proud

Day by day, encompassing the night like she did back in 1776—even to this day.

Thank God for his grace of freedom with flags of our fathers

Chapter 8

Give Love

Give love to one another. Live with a joyful heart, live the part

Give from the heart, no matter what season or time of year. Pick your star, smile—walk that extra mile to dream; aim high, not loud.

Find yourself, love yourself, so you can love others. Uplift others when their life is in a tailspin

Love rules over loss, so when a friend or a lover needs a hug, give a cheerful smile

Some encouragement, be there for them

Give love, love, love, love.

Change the world, your world.

There's world like love from above.

There's no greater gift than love.

Chapter 9

Get Back Up

Looking back on another's love, happiness, heartbreak, joy, sadness, emptiness, loneliness

Captivate my every moment. As I remember you, my child (like a movie), taking me back in time.

I carried you thru birth. I nursed you thru the years. Now, right now, I find myself in a pool of tears. I face fears; you have left me too soon

I'm lost in misery as I face the mirror. Reflection of the past comes to mind. When I know, I held you, love you, kissed you,

When You tested me my child now, I find myself in a pool of tears. I face fears; you have left me too soon

As it's hard to face, knowing I won't get to hold you, kiss you, tell you, show you a mother's love

I'm broken with words unspoken; I wish I'd told you I loved you more. Happiness, heartbreak, joy, sadness, emptiness, loneliness captivate my every moment as I think of you as my child, my child, who left me too soon. I'll see you someday over the moon on the other side.

Until then, I have to GET BACK UP, carry on, carry on, looking back to GET BACK UP to look forward over the horizon.

Chapter 10

I'm a Bowl of Tenderness

I'm a bowl of tenderness, stirring up a commotion of emotion, stirring up feelings, whirling my heart like a Ferris Wheel.

Who Wee! I'm a bowl of tenderness. Cyclone of loneliness—letting go—moving fast forward—take a step back—then

back again toward a captivating heart of Love! Surfing for motion, actions overcoming motive of emotions. My heart is like a pickle. I'm tickled when it comes to loving you. I feel like a tornado making a sweep. I'm past the hiccups with the pickup lines of emotions in my heart. I don't want to be hung up on a clothesline. I want her to be a straight shooter, not a Cowboy Booter! I want some love and tenderness.

Who Wee! I'm a bowl of tenderness. That's right, just like that! Who Wee! Keep It Up, Babe! Going for more—running for Home Plate. Love, in motion, feels so right; it just can't be wrong!

Chapter 11

The Legend of a Cowboy

The young against the old, the open frontier. The Cowboy legend footprints of the West from the top of his ten-gallon hat to the tip of his spurs on his old worn-out boots. Pure instinct of a Cowboy runs through his veins as he holds his bridle reins. A colorful character at his best; even at his worse, he still is a HERO. He could draw his six-shooter from a zero to the HERO, standing the test of caution as he watched his back. The Cowboy was the backbone of the West, traveling free as an Eagle. He rode and traveled the Plains. The Saddle was his cradle. His horse, of course, was his means; his six-shooter was his friend. His domain was the open Prairie out on the Range. Engaged in the trails, he rode singing the Cowboy's songs of old, songs that were told, stories of the cowboys that live to this day. The Legend of a cowboy is here to stay! Getty Up! Join in, Cowboy and Cowgirls. Yippee Ki! Yay, Yippee Ki! Yay, Yippee Ki! Yay, off to cowboy heaven. Mile after mile, the homesick blues till he drops his reins at the end of the trail. He dusts himself off, takes off his boots, and stays a while. (A Cowboy Way.) Till he hits the long, lonesome trail again. Back on the Trail, living a cowboy way.

Chapter 12

"Stupid Today, Stupid Ever in Love"

Stupid today, stupid ever in LOVE. Call on me, talk to me, walk with me. I need your closeness. I need your smile; it lasts me for miles! A frozen moment in time, you are the gold at the end of my rainbow! I long for your touch, always looking for more. I need you. You drive me crazy. Yes, come on drive me crazy. Silly in love. I'm ready, soo ready. Oh, yea! Come on. I'm counting on you to show me. Come hold me. Love me, silly. Till I'm stupid today, stupid ever in LOVE. Let me tell you, whisper in your ear. What your love means to me. You're beautiful, so beautiful. Let your true colors shine. No fear, show your true colors—love me, silly Babe.

Stupid today, stupid ever in LOVE.

Let's believe, live so freely. Stupid today, stupid ever in LOVE.

Stupid today, stupid ever in LOVE (loving it, Babe, Oh, Yea!)

Chapter 13

USA Built by God

Guts, guns, glory! Through sacrifice. No…un…no…un, ACLU. You and me, Freedom for Democracy. Choice Matters. Signs of Freedom stand out. All around you and me. (Our children). It's all in how we raise them that matters for tomorrow's future.

Oh, yes! Oh, no! Oh, yes. (Our children are watching us as parents.) We set examples. The apple in their eye. Against the odds. Chances are, you gave them, or have you given them a stable to be able to stand up, believe in God, and country? For what rights against wrong to believe in true heritage of the USA built by God? Guts, guns, glory! Through sacrifice. No…un…no…un, ACLU.

Chapter 14

Madness Energy, Oh, Dear

Happy-to-sad madness energy, joy to rage, turn the page, engage your emotions to let yourself go, living rich and freely. That's me; your true feelings revealed. Let yourself go madness energy, madness to magic, magic moment; these four walls are closing in on me, and you and I need a breath of fresh air. I'm so ready, so ready to let myself go madness energy. Woo, wee! Oh, yes! I'm on my way so right. I am on my way to Las Vegas. Stop to get gas in Georgia.

I'm a cross-country redneck. I'm squeezed. I'm learning, yes, learning. I'm leaning towards being a country rock hillbilly star fame or fire. Now I am a star time in question. Anybody seen my rose-colored glasses? Feeling good, real good, even when things seem out of place in Mississippi. Missing you, babe. Oh, baby, baby, missing you. I've got the working man blues. Now that I'm a country hillbilly star madness energy, I'm ready, so ready, taking time out to adjust to my ups and downs. I'm ready, so ready to get back home with you, babe, to let go myself. Woo, wee! I'm on my way. Can't you tell madness energy? Oh, baby, next to you, I have madness energy.

Chapter 15

Forgiveness on a Wing and a Prayer

Forgiveness on the wings of a prayer…the best to a burdensome soul. Those who kneel the most stand the best…passed the test…passed the text. Heartfelt humbleness blessings felt and realized grace that only comes from God above.

For those who realize where life begins and never ends with Jesus… Those who kneel the most stumble less…the best passed the test…passed the test, moving forward, moving on, overcoming sin and accepting forgiveness…singing for joy with

Praise to God…forgiveness on the wings of a prayer! Seeking God's face…receiving his loving grace! One to one, one to all. The best that kneeled the most passed the test…passed the test with prayer. All things are possible through Jesus…pure forgiveness, forgiveness, forgiveness, pure forgiveness to the soul. Glory to God for prayer. Yes! Prayer moves mountains…moving on to forgive yourself and others that cause you to have a bruised heart! Forgive so you can be Forgiven… Forgiveness is a responsible act to move forward and move on.

Chapter 16

Meet Somewhere in the Middle

Diamonds, real ones, you heading South. I'm heading north; we meet somewhere in the middle. I'm arrogant; your passion overcomes my arrogance; you're pleading. I'm conceding; you're right; I'm wrong. I'm right; you're wrong. We meet somewhere in the middle. Oh my, you're dripping in them diamonds, real one. Oh, my! You're my Mississippi woman. Oh, yeah! Guess what's cooking up for you, baby! Oh, my. You're my man, rough and tough as nails but gentle as a kitten, old baby. I'm kicking the cat, walking the dog. We'll meet somewhere in the middle, hearts flaming, blaming fire of desire. I'm trying to get past the diamonds, real ones dripping in them.

Chapter 17

Amazing Glory

To God be the glory! Glorify His name; raise your voices and praise, praise His holy name. Praise Him. God gives us something to sing about, so much amazing love—amazing, amazing blessings here and beyond. Amazing power, power, power in the blood of God's Son, Jesus. Jesus Christ is our Lord and Savior. Jesus is the spring of life. Rejoice, rejoicing, very rejoicing, letting Jesus fill you with the true spring of life running from the river of life that flows for all eternity. Glory, glory be to God. Jesus Christ is Lord living, the running river of life that flows for all eternity. Praise Him! Praise Him! Amazing glory!

Chapter 18

Engage in the American Spirit

Engage in the American spirit as traditions stand out through time, touching one's heart too many times through history. History doesn't lie; truth stands out. History that is preserved speaks volumes now to our future as a society, a country, a nation—our heritage. God's love even now remains our heritage. Engage in the American spirit, a rich culture. Set the tone, the very fabric for a nation, a country, the American spirit. So engage in the American spirit when you are called to defend our liberties and our freedoms. Take a stand to preserve. Fight for tomorrow's generations to live and have dreams with love and hope, not despair. To continue to engage in the American spirit, a spirit to prosper. God has wonderfully prospered this nation. Engage in the American spirit.

Chapter 19

God's Sweet Word

God's sweet word, a seed for harvest, touching a soul so pure, oh-so loving, so inviting, so holy, touching and consoling God, sweet word to a soul in need of God's sweet, sweet word—so loving, so inviting, so holy seeds for harvest planted. Praise God! Praise God! Praise be to the Lord! So holy is his sweet, sweet word, such an inspiration both to the same as well as a (truth) true God-ordained path for the unsaved. God's sweet word, so pure! So loving! Oh! So inviting, so holy! Love thy neighbor as thyself! God's sweet, sweet word, teaching us day by day. God's sweet word is so amazing, amazing! He tells us to go and tell His word to any and to all to plant the seeds of salvation far and wide across the landscapes and nations worldwide. God's sweet word (seed for the harvest), lead me, Lord, and I will follow. I feel so humbled to do so. (Tag) Touching a soul. "God's sweet word."

How sweet are your words to my taste, sweeter than honey to my mouth! (Psalm 119:103–104)

Chapter 20

Tip-Tap, Tip-Tap

Tip-tap, tip-tap, fresh surprise! Hip-hop! Hip-hop! Bee bop! Hopping, bee bopping

Toe tapping, adapting to the dance floor… Get rhythm… Get rhythm! Exciting

Atmosphere. To what it can give! Sets the tone…taking it to the limit.

Get down! Get down! Get loud! Hard snapper! Proud toe tapper! Tip-tap! Tip-tap! Do the

Dap! Tip-tap! Tip-tap! This ain't rap… Come on, anybody… Everybody, get down… Get

Down… Get loose! Fancy-free, toe tapping, dancing to the rhythm! Beat of drum working

Work it! Tip-tap! Tip-tap! Do it all together. Tip-eth tap… Toe tapping. Work in progress

That's right! All together—coming together

Chapter 21

A Swing, Miss, No Kiss

A swing, miss, no kiss. What did I miss? Here comes trouble with a rumble nick yack jack! He's out, causing a stir! He lives up to his nickname yackety-yak jack, yackety-yak all the time. Even at half time, all through four quarter's cowboy. What's This? Oh, we have a problem, of course. Actions in question. Foul play! A swing, miss, no kiss! Oh! Nick yack jack would ask, What did I miss! A run-pass a score; a fumble; he's all-time trouble, causing a stir, a rumble; nick yack jack full of yackety-yak yackety-yak with nicknack's coke-jack; jack-coke. His best buddies. So, so sad to see him swing, miss, no kiss. His kissing cousins—cousins: coke-jack, jack-coke, coke, got him in A tornado spin. He's long-winded with loud burps in between. Yackety-yak, jack yackety-yak all the time! A swing, a miss, no kiss—a situation with aggravation with inauguration

Chapter 22

Words of Wisdom

Words of wisdom, no imaginary line so touched with divine love, so moved with your passion so

Enriched with truth, divine words to touch a dying world to enlighten the lesser of the least

No one other than you, Lord, alone to care for one soul to all King of kings Lord of lords, you

Are the Father of mercies so mercifully divine pure love, pure grace to one to all who seek

Your face enriched me, Lord Father, of mercies. Father of lights, your light shines brighter

Than the sun. Shine bright in me, through me. Shine on me and on, for there's no greater light than

Your love, brighter than the sunlight that outshines the darkest. Darkness is covered in

Brightness with your light. O Father, divine of mercies, O Father of light words of wisdom no

Imaginary line, river of glory flowing in me through me. Let it shine! Let it shine! (Words of Wisdom)

Chapter 23

Hearts Eclipse

Heart eclipse! Acceleration of emotions, feelings, feelings encompass my ever being

As I kiss you! You kiss me back! I can't hold back, my true feelings, touching the core of my souls. Oh! So inviting, invigorating with each kiss, with you in my arms. Oh, babe

Kiss me! Kiss me! Till the sunshine of your heart is on fire! And we drift with desire on the waves of the ocean of love. Hearts Eclipse. Touching, touching the stars in the heat of the night, morning rising to the clear, blue sky. In the morning after…still holding…holding on to each other as our Hearts Eclipse.

I've loved you so long, so long with each kiss as our Heart Eclipse.

Chapter 24

Momma's Prayers

A work in progress on the wings of a prayer

Momma prays mystifying doubt, facing momma's beliefs to relieve the burden of crossing the

Bridge of mischief angle of a child with one wing in the fire, charmed by the streets of

Fire momma's patience truly tested and tried; she cried out to God for divine wisdom. She gets down on her knees with a bleeding heart, bleeding heart of love for a child charmed by the streets of fire, ringing down, down, dark shadows

Follows the footsteps of a child with one wing in the fire with running shoestrings are united not fit to be tied stride in motion, causing a mother's heartache thru the years of tears and countless fears. Still, momma prayed. (She fought the devil for her child.) Momma's prayers mystify doubt of a restless angel child. God sees her faith, past emotions, momma's prayers. Momma's prayers kick the fire out of the devil, stepping on his tail as he runs the other way, watching, watching 'em run. (Momma's prayers are answered; a child comes home safe in a mother's arms)

Chapter 25

Four Winds of Tide Blow In

Bazaar events, Times a-ticking shadows. A not-so-normal day. Four winds of tide blowing chances as the day goes on and on. Time doesn't hold back anything for anyone. Anyhow, we stand to be tested, testing ones. Intercool. Bearing a heart of misery as four winds of tide blowing change circumstances changes oneself to another eye-witness, one too many split decisions. Causing hasty motives, crazy ideas, sands of pride, stand between wisdom and fate. Causing hate, grief, mischief, finds, and promise versus compromise. Who's wise? Who's not? Tick-tock. Tick-tock. Around the clock, the four winds of tide blow in changes. Who loses? Who wins? Mix match. Watch the four wins of tide blowing in change, change on the horizon. As the day unfolds, behold. Chances change on and on. Oh, no! Oh, yes. Wisdom overrules. Foolishness, pride facing the four winds of tide. Looking at you to me, I see. Yes, I see the true side of wisdom in the wise verses of foolish pride. How about you? Where do you find yourself standing? The test from the four winds of tide?

Chapter 26

Notebook Diaries

Notebook diaries shallow your life from the sun; you are on the run with a gun.

No fun to live running, taking from the shadows of yesterday, yes, shadows of yesterday

Pride! Notebook diaries—read like a book…when! When you were living and giving!

Now! Now you are all about you! Take steel borrow, not looking for tomorrow to

Find the sun. Your ways of the past don't reflect in the rearview mirror what you're

Leaving behind what you're living now! Why do you do me this way! You cut and run with a gun. You cut me deep to the Core of my very soul. So vain! Now! Now all I have is broken promises, no more roses.

Flower beds with no spring flowers that you once cultivated for me…dreams with thorns go thru flower bed of you and me! Woo-wee… Now noted added to your notebook diaries; you still get to me! You even took my dog, the cat, the sunburnt Chevy pickup. Why, why do you do me this way? Shallow your life from the sun, the price of running with a gun, smokin' at the end of a barrel… bootlegger.

Chapter 27

Talent for Two

Remembering when I caught your scared—mamma mia! Oh, what a night! Precious moments,

Precious memories, precious, precious, just a moment, come to pass... Wauz up,

Darling, you do make my heart sing, skip a beat. I feel something, dreams becoming

Reality, realizing special times together, the times we shared talent for two...

Us two! The show goes on for us! There's no rush to push it! Push it! Talent for two...

We got each other, baby! Oh, yes, baby! Baby! Baby! Your world is my world. My world is

Eclipsed, completed with you! There's nothing better, can you feel it, too? Oh, yes! It just

Doesn't get any better, better than this, just us being the best for each other! Talent for

Two—one plus one equals two! We're a match—strike...soo right! We're just right for

Each other...dreams becoming reality. We put the music in rhythm; we put the light in

The stars! Together! Talent for two...soulmates now and forever...forever

More...that's us. Remember when I told you so... It would be this way someday—that someday is here and

Now remembering its sweet, precious moments, precious memories, precious moments

Continue... I love you! Talent for two...

Chapter 28

He's Always There

When it comes to the script of my life, I'm on stage running with life! Fulfilling, filling

My dreams! My desires, my destiny freedom, freedom from life's shoestrings. I can feel

Freedom! Yes! Freedom, that's me. I'm free! So free! I can do anything, be anything that I want to be.

Oh! Yes! I know there's hope, love, passion. (I know) I'm not standing alone in my

Quest of life's dreams, desires as God is with me in my endeavors even when I

Reach for the stars. He's always there even when I stumble; he's there. He holds

The key to my every care desire of prayer! He's there—always there

To hear my every prayer, whether I'm feeling joyous or sad, I'm glad he's always there!

Jesus is my foundation, my rock. God does let dreams come
True, he's always there, painting me a rainbow of promise
Through Jesus! I got reassurance he's always there.

Chapter 29

Two Lifestyles

(This Song Is Dedicated To [All] My Trucking Buddies! And It Goes Like This!)

Big wheels looking for thrills to kill the chills of Silent, lonely nights; one eye open, the other eye closed

Fighting sleep(midnight rider) bright headlights on Till sunrise turning (18 wheels) to dawn to dust in a

Rush time is money with your honey! I know you want More than bacon strips, honey! Baby! I got to make this

Trip to Amarillo this run. You keep asking me when I'm Going to come home! I'm on this run then I can make a Trip to the house to your gavel driveway! Two Lifestyles on any given day or night! Man, I've been

There! Know that feeling! (The rush is on!) Two Lifestyles bleeding, pleading to please the other: I'm a

Truck-driving fool! I have a redneck disposition, so my Dreams will find a home loved ones calling me back

Home arms wide open memories highlights cherish Times shared for the time at home (3 days) then I'm

Feeling the call of the road! I've got that road fever Calling me away again! Back on the road again! Trip

After trip. Mile after mile (leading and preceding, Proceeding back, back and forth] two lifestyles! Man,

I've been there (know that feeling!)

Chapter 30

Paper Bill of Rights

American Heritage in the Spotlight. The paper in question? American Bill of right activists want changes to our constitution, the 1776 Plan for the people's rights. From our forefathers who wrote down on bone white paper with black ink as we know it as our American. American Constitution, our God-given rights implemented for the people, by the people, for the people.

The good old USA history of the paper has served us well. True generations of issues. Values and morals. Oh. It seems our country has lost some of the true vision of our forefathers, true morals, and values, and our country is bleeding. From not keeping God in our nation. Countries. Schools for our children, our next generation of leaders for tomorrow's generation. Of leaders. The paper Bill of Rights in question for the American people. For the people. By the people. Our American. American Constitution. The paper Bill of Rights. Oh, how? Can it be that we are losing focus on our American heritage?

We are in danger. With opposing activists who are actively active. Taking. The paper. Our Constitution, our rights of the people on the table. Of changed venues versus morals versus venue. Values in question. Who's wrong? Who's right? What's wrong? What's right? The paper Bill of Rights. The right of the people's voices is being. And plead it. What was? Normal seems not normal. What is right? Back when the paper Bill of Rights was implemented. Then is now an activist opposing arguments for his or her. Agenda now to tear. And rewrite the laws of the paper Bill of Rights. True American.

True Americans need to take it. Their voice, voices to the top, pray for America to be. True God's moral nation, a country with dignity, with God-given heritage. Take it. Take it. To stand. To stand. Take your voice to the top hill.

The White House. To Congress. And make a generation. Stand. Stand up. Let the true voice of the people be heard loud and clear for this generation and the future generation to come. The paper. Bill of Rights. The paper. The true voice of the people, for the people, and by the people.

WE THE PEOPLE

About the Author

Born in Fort Campbell, Kentucky, in 1956 and raised in Dallas County, Frank Easterling lived in Central America with his dad and mom, who were stationed in Panama, Central America. He spent two and a half years there and came back to Texas. He finished high school in 1975 and joined the US Army. He was stationed in Korea from 1975 to 1976 and went to Fort Benning, Georgia. He got out of the service in June 1979 and worked in construction for about ten years. Frank got out of construction and moved to Atlas Van Lines. I got my CDL and drove some agents' trucks until he became an owner and operator and got his own tractor lease.

During his time in Atlas Van Lines, he traveled to all forty-eight states, including Canada, and then 9/11 happened. That is when God showed him his talent for writing songs, lyrics, and poetry. Frank got his record. He got to record his first song. The project grew from there, a tribute to our heroes. And he recorded a song. That is, his dad's a true soldier; the first CD, Picture Perfect Test of Times, has twelve songs. One song was "Hero of the Stars." The CD made it to Stafford Air and Space Museum.

In this showcase, an arrow points to song number 8, "Heroes of the Stars," at the Space Museum. It was in the Stafford Air and Space Museum in Weatherford, Oklahoma.

For a limited time and through God's blessings, the song gives tribute to the Columbia Space crew that was lost in the shuttle disaster. Frank also received a letter from President George Bush. He wrote a song lyric for him after 9/11. God is giving him the material to serve him with this talent to share as a ministry. Frank has a CD called Chisholm Trail of Life. Fifteen songs are recorded there, which can also be found today on YouTube. Song placement is numbers 7 and 12. He uses gospel songs on them to reach out to people for Jesus.

STAFFORD AIR and SPACE MUSEUM

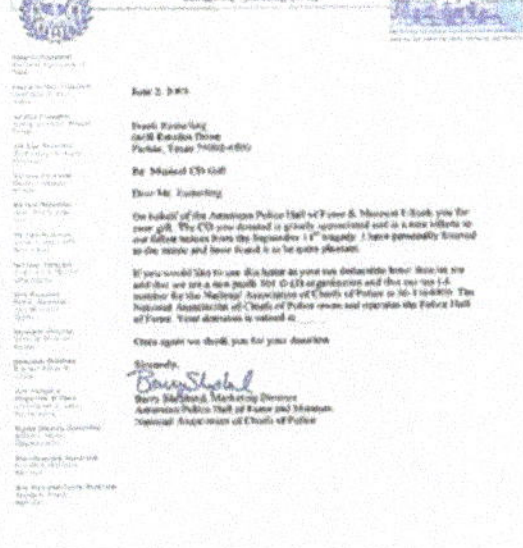

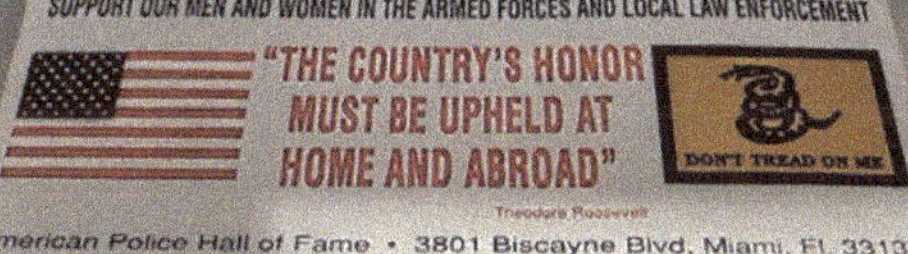

AMERICAN POLICE HALL OF FAME
POLICE MEMORIAL DAY 2001
SUPPORT OUR MEN AND WOMEN IN THE ARMED FORCES AND LOCAL LAW ENFORCEMENT
"THE COUNTRY'S HONOR MUST BE UPHELD AT HOME AND ABROAD"
Theodore Roosevelt
DON'T TREAD ON ME
American Police Hall of Fame • 3801 Biscayne Blvd, Miami, Fl. 33137

CHARLIE DANIELS
3-9-13
DB GUEST

Charlie Daniels
TO FRANK

THE WHITE HOUSE

WASHINGTON

January 6, 2003

Mr. Frank Easterling
6608 Estados Drive
Parker, Texas 75002-6800

Dear Mr. Easterling:

Thank you for your kind words of support.

Serving as President of the United States is an honor, and I
am pleased with the progress we are making in America.
I appreciate your support as we continue to work on issues
that are important to Americans.

Laura joins me in sending our best wishes.

Sincerely,

George W. Bush

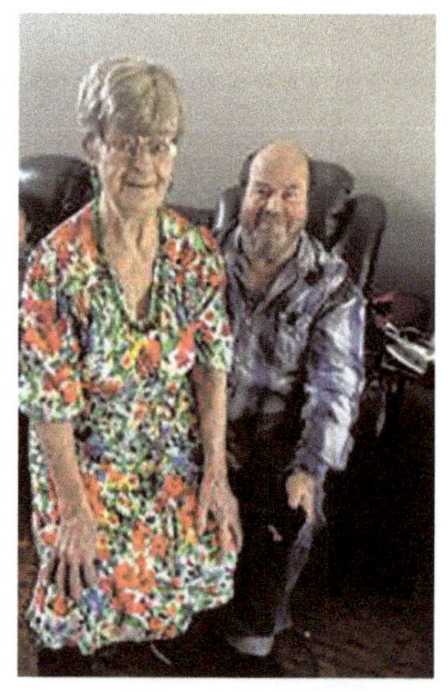